What No One Ever Tells You

What No One Ever Tells You

Selected Works from Underground Writing

Compiled by the Teaching Writers of Underground Writing
Edited by Jennifer Morison Hendrix and Matt Malyon
Cover design by Nathan McGehee

This book is supported, in part, by a grant from the Washington State Arts Commission.

Printed in the United States of America

ISBN 9780999670408
LCCN 2017961640

Underground Writing
P.O. Box 1043
Mount Vernon, WA 98273

www.undergroundwriting.org

Contents

Foreword

Did you ever feel invisible? How about someone you love? Have you seen friends, family or community members, close to your heart, suffer in the shadows, on the fringes, unseen by most of society?

Each short piece in this anthology is a radical act of presence. An assertion of selfhood. Imagine a world where the most voiceless members of our society are given a platform to express their dreams, thoughts, inner strife, love. This anthology not only images such a world, it manifests it.

Some of these authors are undocumented. Others are serving time behind bars. Others are simply trying to get benefits or facing financial hardships. Each, in their own way, faces the oppressive reality of invisibility. These authors may be far from the levers of change, but they have decided to write their truth, and in doing so, they have certainly changed me.

Take the pieces written by incarcerated people. Prisons create, by definition, a system dependent on cultivating opacity and invisibility. They are massive buildings built "over there." Far away from most of our cities and towns. Out of sight, out of mind. Though prisons are full of humans, most of us rarely confront the daily reality for people who are in them. And yet they make up a significant portion of our population—they tell the contemporary story of our nation.

On every page of this book you will find human beings. Taken as a whole, this collection is an instruction manual for how to remember the individual lives and souls trapped in the prison system, in undocumented struggles, and other battles. They are stories that tremble with urgency, vibrancy, and life. They are like literary caffeine, offering a linguistic jolt, chock full of vivid details. The "red metal door" startles me— a sobering image from prison's reality and also a future yet to be decided. Victor's description of his bed: "cold like ice" and the little mirror where "you can't even see yourself." But, oh, Victor— we see you, through your crystalline words. Later, Victor says: "God didn't write beautiful on my heart." A statement that is profoundly beautiful.

A field worker tells us "I see water but it's a mirage." From behind bars, April writes "I am waiting for the fire to dim / The wax to drop / The seal to harden / The letter to send." And though Michael is in juvenile detention, he yearningly remembers where he's from: "the fresh-cooked salmon or the rainstorm coming from the distance."

According to Faulkner, drama is the heart in conflict with itself. These honest, witty, and emotional pieces show us epic internal struggles. There is honesty in these pages: about one's failures and values, one's shadows and beacons. We see individuals wrestling with redemption, culpability, love, family, repentance, and justice.

Writing is freedom, writing is living, writing is celebration, writing is survival, writing is self-actualization. By writing, one becomes visible to the self and to others. These pieces remind us of the pragmatic functionality of storytelling to our democracy.

It is hard to look away from these pieces or un-see them. And so I urge you—spend some time with this book, and don't forget its honesty, its heartbreak, its humanity. Though many of these pieces are laced with sorrow, there is promise here, too. A will to hope and dream one's way to tomorrow. R. writes: "This is my letter to you / do not love or hate me but understand."

Quiara Alegría Hudes
Pulitzer-winning playwright and co-founder of Emancipated Stories

Behind Bars

Wheelbarrels & walking 20s, the daughters
Chasing their father's shadows, sons that upset
The wind with their secrets …

from Reginald Dwayne Betts, "Prison"

I hope time goes by fast while I'm locked up. Damn, I can't wait to get out so I can make some money. Maybe have some fun, hang out with people, be with my family. But most of all I want to munch out hella sick. Oh man, when I get out, I'm going to be a fat boy for a bit.

L.
Skagit County Juvenile Detention

I want to ask for a pencil trick, so I can write down my thoughts.

C.
Skagit County Juvenile Detention

What No One Ever Tells You

What no one ever tells you
is that my dream wasn't to be incarcerated
in Juvenile Detention, nor to be incarcerated
in prison in the future.

What no one ever tells you
is that a dream I once thought about
was to see the whole world, every inch!

What no one ever tells you
is that it's sometimes better not to.

J.S.
Skagit County Juvenile Detention

My Cell

My cell in SCJD has 100 blocks.
There's a red door with a little window, but you can't look outside of the window or you get in trouble.
There's two beds more hard than a rock and cold like ice.
There's a little mirror but you can't even see yourself.

Victor
Skagit County Juvenile Detention

Inside the Juvie Payphone

Going inside the Juvie payphone
You'll find jokes told to keep morale up,
Deep conversations,
So deep it's like you're connecting
With someone you've known for years,
Your life as a matter of fact.

But you also hear the *I'll do better next times,*
The tearful *I'm sorrys,*
The *I love you* from a worried mother.
But then the ten minutes are up
Like the ten minutes it took to write this.

Inside the payphone you hear the push of the numbers
To dial back,
To start a new conversation,
To be happy
Before you go back to your cell.

Cristian
Skagit County Juvenile Detention

After Jasmyne Mendoza, "Go Inside A Beating Heart"

I Have to Swallow the Time

I have to swallow the time
they're gonna try to give me and more,
and if I don't try to swallow, they will force it down my throat.
I have to swallow my family seeing me in an orange jumpsuit.
I have to swallow my responsibilities at a young age,
no messing around, no horseplay.
I have to swallow staring at white walls hours on end.
If I have to swallow one more thing, I think I'm gonna double
over and puke.

If dreams die
I'll feel like the Titanic sinking in all my troubles.
The last thing people will see
are air bubbles.

Cristian
Skagit County Juvenile Detention

After poems composed by Xu Lizhi in a sweatshop and sent via text messages

Rules

1. In a grave.
2. In a hospital.
3. In Juvie…

and it will come fast.
Step into the car and have a seat.
Choose a # 1, 2, or 3!

#3

bed, toothbrush, blankets, 3 meals a day
but I should probably mention, I'm sittin' up in a
Juvenile Detention.

LIFE'S A LESSON TO BE LEARNED SO
MAKE SURE YOU PAY ATTENTION!!!

20-minute visits through glass.
Mother. Misses you and wants you back.

"I told you, don't be doing this, don't be doing that."

J.S.
Skagit County Juvenile Detention

After Jason Reynolds, *Long Way Down*

What No One Ever Tells You

What no one ever tells you
is that "gangbanger" you see walking
down the streets is most of the time a juvenile.

What no one ever tells you
is that the shooting that went down last week
was most likely done by a juvenile.

What no one ever tells you
is that the shooter, and the deceased body
in the news, was most likely a juvenile.

J.S.
Skagit County Juvenile Detention

Four Haiku from Skagit County Juvenile Detention

In my room
reading my book
waiting for rec.

Another day gone.
Another day closer.
Guards getting nosier.

Gun in my hand.
Red or green light.
It's always on sight.

Single file line.
This is my life.
Concrete walls 'til I'm gone.

Anonymous
Skagit County Juvenile Detention

After Tomas Tranströmer, "Nine Haiku from Hällby Young Offenders' Prison"

Three Haiku from Skagit County Juvenile Detention

Hours in my cell
overthinking of when I'll get out
but only time will tell.

It's the same routine every day.
You won't know till you get a taste.
Dreaming, then wishing you'll never wake.

Skylights flashing. Sunlight.
Red doors in my cell.
Is this heaven or hell?

J.S.
Skagit County Juvenile Detention

After Tomas Tranströmer, "Nine Haiku from Hällby Young Offenders' Prison"

I Belong Here

I belong here. Why? For the people I hurt, for the things I did. I stare at the white bricks in my cell feeling angry towards the world, but why? As I start to think, I calm down. Why? Because it is me who put myself here, that's why, I say. I belong here.

I start to have memories of when I was free. All the good times, and I start to feel sad, but then I remember what I've done wrong and who I hurt, and I tell myself…

I belong here.

Alex
Skagit County Juvenile Detention

After Mahmoud Darwish, "I Belong There"

I Am Offering This Poem

I am offering this poem to you
since I have nothing else to give.
Remember it like you would your first kiss,
or like a present that money can't buy.
Wondering when it's my time to die,
looking at white walls all day, walking in a single file line,
hands behind my back, wishin' I could go back.
Red doors, never again. I ain't coming back no more.
Only 16, with a lot to see....

Anonymous
Skagit County Juvenile Detention

After Jimmy Santiago Baca, "I Am Offering This Poem"

I Write in Order To

I write in order to
express myself not to
comprehend myself. I'm
not ashamed to admit that
I can't say the stuff I write,
for I am ashamed what
people will think. I often
look at myself when I
am washing my face
in the sink, and I start
to think what's the meaning
to this place
to wake up
to fall asleep
just to wake up again
and do the same thing.

Alex
Skagit County Juvenile Detention

After Anna Kamieńska, "The Lamp"

I Won't Front

I won't front.
It sucks sleeping day by day in these Juvie bunks.
But seems like there's more good in here
than there is out there.
It's like I turned over my freedom for some knowledge.

J.S.
Skagit County Juvenile Detention

After Jason Reynolds, *Long Way Down*

My Heart is Pumping

My heart is pumping blood
So that is blood circulation
But don't get it mistaken
You are my heart
So there, you are my motivation!

We are the ones who get mad when we
Have to go back to our rooms.
Because "time's up." We are waking up every day
Not to our own freedom but our individual
    judgment days.
We are the ones who are trippin' on how the prosecutor
Is trying to do us dirty, knowing she can.
We are the ones who can't do anything
But wait for the outcome.

Cristian
Skagit County Juvenile Detention

After Anna Akhmatova, *Requiem*

Left Out

...maybe they'll take us
to another detention center we'll eat we'll have a floor
a blanket toilets water and each other
for a while.

from Juan Felipe Herrara, "Borderbus"

I am terrified of my dad one day fully being gone and leaving me, of being so alone, knowing the person I could count on is now gone, and I am alone.

M.
Skagit County Juvenile Detention

I Am a Field Worker and I Am Tired

I am a field worker and I am tired
I wonder if they are going to change the rules
I hear voices planning to march
I see water but it's a mirage
I want to be rich
I am a field worker and I am tired
I pretend to work so I don't get kicked out of the fields
I feel tired of working and my back hurts
I touch water
I worry for my mom and my little sisters
(who are like my kids)
I get frustrated and cry because my kids do bad stuff
I am a field worker and I am tired
I am polite to my kids when they listen
I understand when my kids get in trouble
I tell my sisters to get a good job
I dream that the world is going to be better
I try to do my best
I hope that someday people get paid equally
I am a field worker and I am tired

Juan
Migrant Leaders Club

After Juan Felipe Herrera and *DreamFields: A Peek into the World of Migrant Youth* (2012)

I Belong Here Because

I am from an immigrant background.
I belong here because
I came here to accomplish my goal,
which is to make my mom proud of me.
I belong here because
I am going to make a difference.
I belong here because
I am going to tell you my story.

Esmeralda
Migrant Leaders Club

Dear ICE

I've known of your existence from the time I was four years old. You were always told to me

like a scary story, something from a dark fairy tale. But one day you came for us. You knocked

on the front door and put my father in shackles. When I saw you, I knew the monsters were real. You dislocated my family for years, and I still think of you daily.

One question I always have for you: How can you live with yourself?

Adriana
YMCA Oasis Daylight Center

Students had been reading work about immigration issues, including pieces written by members of the Migrant Leaders Club.

Dreams

I have had many dreams throughout my years.
I dreamed I would visit my dad.
I dreamed my family would get papers.
I dreamed I would be able to go to Mexico.
I dreamed that my dad would be with my family forever.

But now my dream is to be an architect
and take care of my mom.

Eloisa
Migrant Leaders Club

After Juan Felipe Herrera and Langston Hughes

I Have Parents

I have parents who go through oppression. My mother is an extremely intelligent woman who is oppressed to both take care of the house and work because she is a "woman." She wants to be educated but is neglected by the ghost of words that tell her she can't. My father is a man who lives in the past, a place in which girls are slaves of men, and men of society. No matter what we say it's hard to change. But we have a chance. I am a girl who knows she is capable.

Rocio
Migrant Leaders Club

Written in response to a prompt about a future in which life has somehow changed. The students had been discussing a scene from Alan Haehnel's play, *The Long View*.

Society Weighs Me Down

Society weighs me down
like a boulder on my back.
For me, being judged
because I am not good looking
or because I'm thin
and don't have big muscles…
to some people it might seem
like the weight is nothing.

Xaiviar
YMCA Oasis Daylight Center

What No One Ever Tells You

What no one ever tells you,
they say behind your back,
but never to your face.

What no one ever tells you,
they show you,
actions speak louder than words.

What no one ever tells you
is what you don't wanna hear.
They say what you wanna hear.

Anonymous
Skagit County Juvenile Detention

My Life Has Been Difficult

My life has been difficult because I've mostly grown up without both of my parents and siblings, basically my whole family. I was homeschooled, which was hard for me because I didn't have any friends. I wasn't allowed to talk to people in the streets, or even family members.

Martha
Migrant Leaders Club

Students had been discussing immigration.

The Hardest Thing for Me to Understand

I think the hardest thing
for me to understand is that my life
has been difficult, and in many different ways.
My family has been through a lot…
and I know that I am barely a kid, that I shouldn't worry about
it, but I do. And I will keep worrying
until I know that my family is safe and ok.

Esmeralda
Migrant Leaders Club

Dear America

1

You have the power to do whatever
you want to do.

I just want to let you know that whatever
you do you do it on your own.

One day you gonna find out that everything
that you're doing is not cool.

Why do you care about the color of people?
What does color do to you?

I know that people mess up
but look at you.

Victor
Skagit County Juvenile Detention

Written the day after the 2016 election in response to works by Bob Dylan, James Baldwin, Langston Hughes, and Denise Levertov.

2

I say this sincerely. You are good.
People with red-hot hands have
scorched your previously lush skin.
People with steel-toed boots kicked
over people who lived here peacefully
to build a meaningless monetary
value empire. This wasn't your fault, and the
majority of people that lay upon you are good.
But America, people try to be bigger than you.
They want it all to themselves.
What will you do about this?

Heather
YMCA Oasis Daylight Center

3

Why are you trying to kick us out?
We know that we entered the States illegally, but we did it
because we wanted a better future than we had in Mexico.
We are the ones who pick your fruits and vegetables—
without us you wouldn't have your fresh fruits and
vegetables.

Marcela
Migrant Leaders Club

4

Why do you hate yourself?
We hate because of the color of our skin, and
sexual preference, calling each other faggots,
wetbacks, lowlifes, worthless.
Why do you hurt yourself?
We shoot up schools, rip children from
their crying mothers, rape, use,
abuse, and cry ourselves to sleep.
Dear America, can't you see that
we're all human?
If you prick us we bleed, tickle us we laugh.
We love, we lose, we cry, we dance and sing.
A black man still has a heart.
A Mexican woman has warm blood running
through her veins.
An Asian man can sing about what he
loves about this country despite all the hate.
Dear America, what do you love about yourself?

Destery
YMCA Oasis Daylight Center

After "Dear America" poems by other Underground Writing students

Think of Us

You may forget but
Let me tell you
this: someone in
some future time
will think of us[*]

Sappho, "Fragment 60"*

I enjoyed being able to just let some of my feelings out. I'm the type who doesn't talk about feelings at all.

C.
Skagit County Juvenile Detention

This is my letter to you – do not love or hate me but understand.

R.
Skagit County Juvenile Detention

---

* Sappho, "Fragment 60," trans. Mary Barnard (1986), California-Princeton; reissue edition.

What No One Ever Tells You

What no one ever tells you
is that they're hurting.
No one tells you
about their dark side
they try to put a mask
on their emotions.

What no one ever tells you
is their true feelings
either good or bad.
They hide feelings
they are embarrassed of.

What I never want to tell you
is goodbye. I want to last forever.
I never want to eventually
forget you or what you look
like. I never want to
see your smile torn into a frown.

Xaiviar
YMCA Oasis Daylight America"

I Am Not Who You Think I Am

I did bad things
Everyone does bad things

I am not perfect but
No one's perfect

But it doesn't mean that
I can't be like you

I don't have money or a good
Car like you but I can work
Hard like you and buy one

We're all the same if we
Work hard we can have

The same things

Victor
Skagit County Juvenile Detention

After Walt Whitman, *Leaves of Grass* and Langston Hughes, "I Too, Sing America"

My Life

I'm from Mount Vernon, Washington. I went to school in different cities in Skagit. I write this in SCJD, while I wear orange, not because I like it. It's because I have to. I hate this color because I see it every day. It stands out too much, like a bright pumpkin. I'm writing this to get my message to you and to let you know I'm not the crook the county labels me as. I'm the quiet, soft-spoken kid. Where I'm from you can't let people know you're soft-spoken because some might think you're not "hard," you're broken. Walking down there knowing there's gonna be a fight and peace of mind is never in sight. I'm sixteen, by the way. Simple is not in my life, but hey, that's okay. Instead I have hardship and sorrow,
the type where if I go to sleep, it won't be gone tomorrow.

Cristian
Skagit County Juvenile Detention

This poem was part of *Film Verse*, a collaborative project between Underground Writing and Voices of the Children, which used writings from Skagit County Juvenile Detention as the inspiration for short films directed by Mount Vernon High School students. The short film for this poem is available for viewing on the Underground Writing website.

My Voice Ran Away

My voice ran away
and wears a mask
to hide its true
identity. No one knows
what's under it, only
me. I don't show what's
under it for fear of
it going away completely.

Xaiviar
YMCA Oasis Daylight America"

Home in Washington

Swinomish
    I am from this tribe.
Skagit
    I live in this county.
Canoe journey
    Every summer my tribe attends this journey.
Pow wows
    When the canoe journey is over, my family and I go to the Yakama pow wows with what's left of my summer (RIP).
My father
    Alexander Jr. Paul from Skagit County Singers Pow Wow group.
Fry bread
    Indian tacos. My favorite food back at Yakama. I want to learn how to make it.

Michael
Skagit County Juvenile Detention

After Alexie

I Am Different Than You Think

I am different than you think.

I am a girl who's been experiencing a sad life at a young age.

I am a girl who hides her feelings.
I am a girl who would seem happy.

I don't have a happy family like I did before. You think I have a loving mom and dad, but my dad passed away, and I am different inside.

Eloisa
Migrant Leaders Club

After Janet, "You See Me as Trouble" in *Dream Fields: A Peek into the World of Migrant Youth* (2012)

If I Were to Live My Life

If I were to live my life
Way back deep in the past
Would you call me a savage?
Would I even last?
As my elders would say, I'm a young
Warrior at war with my heart
My life is like a beautiful art.
Or, my life is like a puzzle
Always trying to find the last part.

Luciean
Skagit County Juvenile Detention

I Am Not What You Think I Am

I am not what you think I am.
I'm not a monster
who likes to fight
and I ain't just
a druggy from the streets.
I used to be good
I used to be chill
but now I'm changing
trying to do better.
I don't see how
you can't see.

Luciean
Skagit County Juvenile Detention

After Walt Whitman, *Leaves of Grass* and Langston Hughes, "I, Too, Sing America"

What's Written in the Heart

I've seen the sun fall from the sky to kiss
the moon goodnight over 300 times.
Us as people, the times, we flow like water.
Ideas come and go, but we stay and grow.
Those who stay static get lost and become obscure.
Father, your daughter doesn't want no man.
She can stand on her own two feet.
Mother, your son is handy with a needle,
doesn't want no construction job.
Yes, we flow like water into new streams.
This is a new stage.
The times they be a changin'.

Destery
YMCA Oasis Daylight Center

After Bob Dylan, "The Times They Are A-Changin'"

I Celebrate Myself

I celebrate myself by either resting or reading a really long book. Sometimes I just sit on my bed and think about tomorrow's plans or maybe do push-ups while counting to 8,000 on my breathing. At school I always practice typing. If I'm not typing then I work on my history. That's what I like about my life. Thank you for listening.

Michael
Skagit County Juvenile Detention

After Walt Whitman, "Song of Myself"

A Day So Happy

Kicking back at my pad

Looking at the sky

Thinking about my self

Who I really am

The kid who everyone thinks is bad
Or the good kid I want to be

My homies said, *You down homes?*

Good people said, *Look at the criminal*

But I think I'm a good kid.

Victor
Skagit County Juvenile Detention

After Czeslaw Milosz, "A Gift"

We, Too, Sing America

Each singing what belongs to him or her and to none else,
The day what belongs to the day – at night the party of young fellows, robust, friendly,
Singing with open mouths their strong melodious songs.

Walt Whitman, "I Hear America Singing" from *Leaves of Grass*

I am the darker brother.
They send me to eat in the kitchen
When company comes,
But I laugh
And eat well…

from Langton Hughes, "I, Too, Sing America"

The Salish Sea

We are America
Whitman and Hughes
spoke of the beauty of this great land
and shook it for its flaws. I live
by my love, the Salish Sea. And here
I hear all of us sing, be it a darker brother
that speaks of dreams, or the screams
of liberty at the steps of our great front door.
Here in this land that was all about liberty,
we are free to sing of our own America.
This is the home that I love and live in
by the Salish Sea.

Kioni
Skagit County Community Justice Center

After Langston Hughes, "I, Too, Sing America"

I Am of the Adopted

I, too, sing America.
I am of the adopted.
I am on the fringe of society.
I struggle, I breathe.
I care, I feel forgotten.
The police, they arrest me.
The doctors, they diagnose me.
But my heart sings my song
as the world passes by.
My hope will prevail
though I still live outside.

Joshua
Skagit County Community Justice Center

After Langston Hughes, "I, Too, Sing America"

I Sing America in Hospital Beds

I, too, sing America
in hospital beds,
wires stuck to my skull
with heavy glue.
In an office,
checking "yes" to
"disability," clarifying,
"I have epilepsy but—"
they aren't listening after that,
the "I have," the "yes."

I, too, sing America.
In my nightmares of
fire and threats the news
eagerly shares.

In school, working ahead,
because if the medicine
fails, I can't take back the time.
I, too, sing America—
they hear "epilepsy" and
pretend they can't hear me.

Ally
YMCA Oasis Daylight Center

After Langston Hughes, "I, Too, Sing America"

This Is My America

This is my America.
Even stripped bare of my rights,
losing face and dignity.
Even trying to take my self-respect.
But I refuse to surrender
what small pieces of myself I have left.
They can take all I have,
until nothing material is left.
But my mind is much stronger
than their abuse and disrespect.
So I wait for the day
the judge sets me free
to build my own America
and show those bastards
just exactly what I can be.

Joel
Skagit County Community Justice Center

After Langston Hughes, "I, Too, Sing America"

I, Too, Am ~~American~~ Native

I, too, am ~~American~~ Native.
These are my ancestral grounds.
Here my sacred drums pound,
equal to every race,
although never enslaved,
spilled ancestral blood
for game and furs.
Now on reservations,
casinos and gas stations.

Dennis
Skagit County Community Justice Center

After Langston Hughes, "I, Too, Sing America"

Tryna Do What's Right

I, too, am American, but it seems sometimes
like I'm from a different race, the prosecutor
treating me like I'm an alien from a different
world, trying to keep me behind bars some
of my life. Even though I know what I did
wasn't right, but he don't care. So, I try
to carry light, going to sleep every night,
tryna do what's right.

Anonymous
Skagit County Juvenile Detention

After Langston Hughes, "I, Too, Sing America"

The Last Candle

I, too, sing America,
the hushed whispers in the sea of song.
A population growing, left no attention knowing,
that help will never come.
A paraded flag is showing that help has come at last,
a flag flown high, but no deeper founded than
a pharaoh's grave at night.
We hear a new one coming,
a sinking boat on land.
The crew's all here, we speak and cheer,
as we freeze to death tonight.
The last candle is now burning.
The final songs are turning.
At least we bought some time.

Xavier
YMCA Oasis Daylight Center

After Langston Hughes, "I, Too, Sing America"

In Dark Places

Placing a book in my hands, the angel said, "It holds all you would wish to know." And he vanished.
So I opened the book, which wasn't thick.
It was written in an unknown alphabet.

from Paul Veléry, "The Angel Handed Me a Book"

She is weeping for her lost right arm.
The stump aches, and her side.

from Denise Levertov, "Weeping Woman"

Since then, my ladders
only climb down,
and all the earth has become a house
whose rooms are the hours…

from Li-Young Lee, "Little Father"

I Have This Idea in My Head

I have this idea in my head that you have to be born beautiful
in order to dream beautiful things. God didn't write
beautiful on my heart. I'm stuck with all my bad dreams.
Bad dreams for bad boys. I guess that's the way it is for me.

I keep having this dream. It's like being in hell. I know
this dream…but it still scares me because there's always
a monster lurking in the dark. The monster wants me dead.
I wonder if I'm the only one who has a monster.
It's just a dream.

I have been running forever…
It's night and the monster is running.
He's trying to get me, and I don't know why…
It's just a dream.

Victor
Skagit County Juvenile Detention

After Bob Dylan, "It's Alright, Ma (I'm Only Bleeding)," Langston Hughes, "I, Too, Sing America," and Denise Levertov, "Weeping Woman"

Dear System

Ever since I was born you've been there. You were there when my biological mom would relapse and let my sister and I run around free. You were there again as I began to realize how to work on my own and take care of my mom and little sister. You were there when my biological dad went into a rage and hit someone. You were there when my mom used up her last chance. You took me and my little sister from her. You weren't there when I was passed from family member to family member. You were there to give me to a new family. You were the ones who put both my parents in jail. You put my biological dad in prison. Now you are here again, but this time just for me. You are here putting me in Juvenile Rehabilitation for the same reason my biological dad's locked up. You've brought nothing but pain in the fourteen years I've known you. You have torn apart my family time and time again only to put me in a new one where I've done nothing but disappoint or make people angry. So, System, before I finish this letter, I just want to say that I will never forgive you.
Sincerely,
Robert

Robert
Skagit County Juvenile Detention

After James Baldwin, *The Fire Next Time*

The Book Was Fat and Big

The book was fat and big, it was all my life in it.

I had my life in my hands. It was my only time to change it. I closed my eyes for a moment to think what I wanted to do.

I opened my eyes back up and the book was on fire. I saw the black smoke in the sky and the book was gone.

Victor
Skagit County Juvenile Detention

After Paul Valery, "The Angel Handed Me a Book"

How Many

How many times have I done something wrong? Must be a lot because I almost remember them all. How many times have I done dope? Too many to count and that's no joke. How many times have I hurt the people I love most? That is something I will never know.

Luciean
Skagit County Juvenile Detention

After Bob Dylan, "Blowin' in the Wind"

What No One Ever Tells You

What no one ever tells you
is about the dreams they have
when they sleep, about how
they never want to go back to sleep
in fear of those dreams.

What no one ever tells you
is about how they dream the future,
cause they can never tell.

What no one ever tells you
is the dream they had about you,
in fear of it actually happening.

Anonymous
Skagit County Juvenile Detention

My Mind Is in the Dark

My mind is in the dark
sitting on the bathroom floor
blood is flowing down my arm
brown is in my veins
I'm nodding, my mind is going
insane. My brain is dying
but I don't feel the pain
On the inside I'm crying
my heart is full of shame
in my mind I always want more no one knows how I feel
life doesn't even feel real

Luciean
Skagit County Juvenile Detention

Thinking...

So I'm in deep depression now
There's nothing I can do about it
I've been sleeping all day
I get real tired when I'm this way.
I start thinking and thinking
And my mind goes crazy.
I get the same thought
Over and over—
What would things be like if
I ended my life today?
I stare, and I stare.
I think about everyone
Who loves me, hates me,
Who wouldn't care
If I just disappeared one day.
I think and I think—
Wouldn't it be better if it all
Just went away?

Sophia
Skagit County Juvenile Detention

Written in response to a dialogue about honesty and a discussion of various texts, including writings of Raymond Carver and Emily Dickinson.

Stars

When you visit me, I feel small. Having you so close makes my body burn and blister. I wish your light could fill my heart instead of darkening my brain. You and all your siblings hold so much beauty inside yourselves and make my beauty and unique features seem void and dull. Hold me with your cold light and take away my meaning. Your visits make my heart shine with hope and my brain drown in useless thoughts. I wish I didn't miss you. You don't even know my name. But I can name every twinkle in your eye, each freckle on your cold, lifeless body. I'll see you tonight if the clouds allow. I look forward to our thoughtless time together. Save me a spot in your next life.

Love,

Someone who doesn't matter

Eddy
YMCA Oasis Daylight Center

After Robert Rottet, "Reverb"

Beef

Ain't the kind you eat, ain't the kind you enjoy
when you're hungry.
It is the kind you have with more people
than calories in a quarter-pounder,
the kind when it starts, it doesn't end,
the kind you ain't enjoy...
          I need less calories.

Anonymous
Skagit County Juvenile Detention

After Jason Reynolds, *Long Way Down*

The Night Is Young, So Am I

Smoke, it flying, and my lungs don't die
Being high was life, used to think I could fly
Now I'm stuck in a cell

Thinkin' of life
Days are goin' forever

So slow
My life's like a totem pole

But what comes next,
I will never know
Let's hope I don't get stuck
In a cell that I will always know

Luciean
Skagit County Juvenile Detention

The Best Drug

At the beginning, someone convinces you to try it
And you like it.

You think about it all the time.
You crave it; you want it
More than anything.
You spend all your money on it

And it becomes
A bigger and bigger part of your life.
You can't live without it.
Suddenly, it's pulled away from you.
You can't have it anymore.
You go through painful withdrawals.
You curse yourself for picking it up in the first place.
But you still want it back.
After a while, you say to yourself,

I'm glad I'm off. I'm never going back.
But most everyone relapses.
The cycle starts over.
Love. Everyone is fighting to get a little.

Sophia
Skagit County Juvenile Detention

One Medicine I've Taken

One medicine I've taken is a drug
But not the legal kind.
The kind that act legal,
almost feel legal.
The medicine that I get
Is from the doctor on the street.
Instead of a pill bottle it's in a bag.
Instead of a doctor he's a thug.
This medicine is better
and even cheaper.
It makes the pain go away
like medicine is supposed to,
right? I feel instantly better.
Even though I could die.

M.
Skagit County Juvenile Detention

After Martín Espada, "My Father As a Guitar"

NASCAR Dialogue

I was lying in bed on the phone in the middle of the night. "So what you want to talk 'bout?" I said.

She was silent for a while then said, "Nascars. They're mesmerizing! They go left, then left again," she said.

I was staring at the ceiling a while before I said, "You're a strange one, aren't you?" She agreed and we both started laughing. The rest of the night we were complaining about stupid things until I fell asleep.

Josh
Skagit County Juvenile Detention

After Hal Sirowitz, a dialogue poem

Hey

Hey, babe. I was thinking about you the other day. I was thinking about the first day that you talked to me. I was feeling like if I was in a movie or something like that, the way that you talk to me when you started laughing, I felt like if I was flying the sky.

Victor
Skagit County Juvenile Detention

After Osip Mandelstam, "Night Piece," and Marina Tsvetaeva, "A kiss on the forehead"

Trying to Catch Up to You

I sit here on my bed looking out my window.
I see fields that stretch as far as the eye can see.
A blue sky the sun is shining white fluffy clouds dot the sky.
I remember the time we were wandering around
    out in the county roads.
You were standing there waiting patiently for me
with that goofy smile. Your golden-brown hair
    shining in the sun.
I'm trying to catch up to you.
As I get closer you wrap your arms around me
    I hug your waist.
Put my head on your chest. This is my safest place
    in whole world.
I feel the warmth of your body I close my eyes
    to hear your heart beat.
I think about our future we will build together,
watching our beautiful daughters grow into beautiful women
Me and you growing old together.
Then as you pull your arms back and cup my face
    with your big hands,
I'm brought back from my thoughts.
Then you smile at me with that smile again.
Say, "I love you, baby."
But then my heart starts to hurt as the reality hits me again.
Then there I am again staring out the window.
Trying to catch up to you.

Janice
Skagit Valley Recovery Community
After Martha Serpas, "Lying in the Middle of the Field"

An Orange to My Nephew

The orange that was given to me by my uncle who said, "Here have an orange, it will help you later in life," which it did on the weekend my nephew was sick, and I told him what his Grandpa said to me, that two oranges would make you well. But his parents didn't have any money, so after my visit with my nephew, I went to the gas station and bought him two orange juices.

Michael
Skagit County Juvenile Detention

After Gary Soto, "Oranges"

After Every Phone Call

After every phone call
I just want to fall
When I hang up
I feel stuck
Wishing I could have spoken up
And say thank you for still being in my life
After all the dumb and pointless fights
That led to sleepless nights
And I want to say I'm ok
I'm sorry after all the chances I had
I passed my time thinking I will get another chance
But now I'm stuck
In a cell feeling out of luck.

As I imagine this reaching you, I see that smile
From eye to eye
And just by seeing that
It made your forgiveness clear.

Cristian
Skagit County Juvenile Detention

After Paul Callus, "Unspoken Words"

Things Are Arising in Me

All the mishaps
The should've
The would've
But no excuses except the drugs
The stupid, mind-numbing drugs
All the things I should've done
All the things I should've, would've had
All for you
For me, for my kids, our lives
I don't like the feelings.
The guilt
The shame
The doubts
The fears
I don't like being reminded that you were so good to me
and I was the piece of shit that you called yourself.

April K.
Skagit County Community Justice Center

After Matthew Siegel, "Sometimes I don't know if I'm having a feeling"

I See You

I see you in my daughter's eyes,
in the expressions my son makes.
I see you in the swaying branches,
and the ripples upon the lake.
I see you when I look in the mirror,
and I miss you all the more.
I see you in the break of dawn,
when the sun rises over the shore.
I see you in the nighttime sky,
where the moon and stars collide.
I see you in the ocean blue,
where the water fluctuates with the tide.
Oh Daddy, how I miss you so
and I feel so very lost.
Never did I realize how much
those missed moments with you cost.

Tiffany
Skagit Valley Recovery Community

After Nichita Stănescu, "In Praise of People"

Survival

Watching the pole ring and tug
My Dad stands above me
Guiding me to reel in a fish
Like a bear guiding his cub
To one day be on their own.

M.
Skagit County Juvenile Detention

After Martín Espada, "Tiburon"

Dear Grandpa

I know we probably never met but I wish we did. I will always remember that one first and last phone call, where you told me two things, "*Mija, Nelly significa estrella,*" and "*La flor mas hermosa eres tú porque el estambre es tu familia, los petalos tus amigos, y el sentro tú.*"

Nelly
Migrant Leaders Club

Students had been reading "Dear …" poems written by other students in Underground Writing workshops.

Posole

My favorite traditional food is *posole*.

A good memory I have is when me and my family celebrate *Dia de los muertos*

Me and my sisters put it out and wait for our dead relatives to come,

or our living ones to come,

and celebrate with us.

Anonymous
Migrant Leaders Club

The People Who Influenced My Life

The person who influenced me the most is my mom.
My mom has taught me many things throughout
my life. She has told me to do well in school
and to go above my education. My mom
is a brave and strong and caring person.
She has said she loves all races
no matter how they look
but the way they act.
She has worried all
her life, and I
will do the
same for
her.

Eloisa
Migrant Leaders Club

We Sit Here Together

We
Are all in Juvie.
We
All sin.
We
Laugh and awkwardly grin.
We
Write in our notebooks.
We
Are all wearing orange.
We
Just bored.
We
Just sleep.
We
Roaming the dark night
We

Students and Teaching Writers, in a circle, one line each
Skagit County Juvenile Detention

After Gwendolyn Brooks, "We real cool"

Where I'm From

I'm writing this poem for my Uncle Kevin back at home in Swinomish, which is the tribe I've lived in since I was 6 years old. Two days after I was in here, my uncle had a stroke; it made me care for him. I care about my family.

In Swinomish, I live with my uncle and auntie, Kevin and Pat. Some of the things I taste, sense, hear, and see are the fresh cooked salmon or the rainstorm coming from the distance. The fresh taste of smoked salmon right off the fire, and the cooked fry bread that my auntie made for the pow wow in Swinomish as a snack. I also hear the singing from our Journey songs, but most of all I see my home, the Swinomish Tribe.

One of my strongest interests is football and my family knows how much I like football. Another couple of things I like are dancing, singing, cooking, watching movies, playing video games, but most of all is being with my family.

Michael
Skagit County Juvenile Detention

This poem was part of *Film Verse*, a collaborative project between Underground Writing and Voices of the Children, which used writings from Skagit County Juvenile Detention as the inspiration for short films directed by Mount Vernon High School students. The short film for this poem is available for viewing on the Underground Writing website.

I Am Waiting

I am waiting for the fire to dim
The wax to drop
The seal to harden
The letter to send
The words to be read
The feelings to resonate
The emotions to unfold
The tears to flow
The love to embrace
The warmth to be felt
You at my side
Always and forever
I am waiting

Ashley
Skagit County Community Justice Center

After Lawrence Ferlinghetti, "I Am Waiting"

A New Chapter

Hold back, men of Ithaka, from the wearisome fighting,
so that most soon, and without blood, you can settle
everything.

from Homer, *The Odyssey* (Lattimore, trans.)

So I learned that poems start flowing more easily after I start writing them, which is really frustrating because I don't have a pencil in my room and it's hard to retain all of the poetry that I write in my head. But I'm grateful for these classes and rec., when I can write them down as they come out.

J.
Skagit County Juvenile Detention

Reading and distractions only bring you so far…when I'm writing it opens me up. Trips me out, too. I didn't know I could look so deep into myself.

T.
Skagit County Community Justice Center

To Myself When I Get Out

Ok, listen up, buddy. When you get out things aren't going to be all happy unicorns and rainbows; it's going to be hard. You're going to have to do you own laundry and make your own food. No more of this institutionalized [blank] anymore! Your [blank]* is in the real world! I expect you to act like a mature adult! You can handle this. I know you can. Don't go back to drugs 'cause that's the [blank] that got you stressed in the first place. Handle. Your. Self.

Josh
Skagit County Juvenile Detention

After Jimmy Santiago Baca, "Letters Come to Prison"

*Skagit County Juvenile Detention policy dictates that students refrain from using "bad language." This student writer developed the [blank] convention.

Journeying

I am journeying back toward a place of peace. It's gonna be hard. It's gonna be a struggle. I'm gonna follow my heart so don't mess with me devil 'cause God is on my side. Get up on my level. I hope I make it safe and don't even struggle. You'll see. Back home happy on a whole 'nother level.

Luciean
Skagit County Juvenile Detention

After Homer, *The Odyssey*

What No One Ever Tells You

What no one ever tells you
is that talent isn't "natural talent."
You have to build it from nothing
like a house, and in the end, it will protect you
either in one or various ways.

What no one ever tells you
is the master was once a beginner,
that every road no matter how long
starts and ends like winter and spring,
like the sun rising and setting.

What no one ever tells you
is that love is like a lake.
You can drown, and it may be cold,
it harbors life, and it can dry up,
or it can flood and destroy its surroundings.

What no one ever tells you
is that you should think about everything
you do because you won't be able to
change them. They will stick
with you like leeches.

What no one ever tells you
is that the more you sit around
and do nothing, the more opportunities
you are missing, the more impacts
you could have made to help, swirl
down the drain like liquid gold.

What no one ever tells you
is that your destiny is not already chosen.
It's only yours to control, by your choices,
the now—neither present nor past. The future
is an empty canvas of your destiny.

Brandon
Skagit County Juvenile Detention

I Am Waiting

I am waiting to go back home
To reunite with my children and husband
I am waiting for my court date to come up
To figure out what's going to happen with myself
I am waiting for God to answer my prayers
And fill my desire to hug and kiss my children again
I am waiting for my lawyer to come visit me
And tell me some good news
I am waiting in a jail cell, for my soon
freedom and liberty
I am waiting for new beginnings to start
So I can begin a new chapter in my life
I am waiting for that moment when the
Guards tell me to pack up my stuff, because
I will finally be heading home to never
separate from my children and husband again

April B.
Skagit County Community Justice Center

After Lawrence Ferlinghetti, "I Am Waiting"

What Can Purge My Mind

What can purge my mind
What can purge my heart
of the sorrow and sadness they feel.
The sorrow from the beast inside
my mind.
The sadness from the people inside
my heart.
Only you, my glowing guide,
Can help purge me of this pain inside.
You tear down my walls of fear
and plant seeds of trust and comfort.
The garden you've built around my
broken mind has grown and flowered.
Weaving between my damaged thoughts
And memories.
Filling and repairing them,
healing takes time.
But your garden of compassion has
set the process in motion.
The process of purging me of
my insecurities and unwanted,
altered emotions.

Eddy
YMCA Oasis Daylight Center

Five Things I Want to Do

1. Spread positive feedback to those in need.
2. Love everyone unconditionally.
3. Help to the best of my ability.
4. Make myself better for others.
5. Warm people's hearts with my smile and dumb jokes.

Zach
YMCA Oasis Daylight Center

I Am Waiting

I'm waiting for a date, waiting for a time.
For life, a life without barriers and with all calm and peace
A life without worry, shame or blame.
A life full of love, full of laughter and smiles.
Full of food.
Never hungry.
Never forgotten.
Never hate.
Full of passion, full of inspiration.
I'm waiting for a life of meaning and purpose.
A life lived in waiting for a start.

April K.
Skagit County Community Justice Center

After Lawrence Ferlinghetti, "I Am Waiting"

Potential

I sit in a grief-stricken house

mindlessly pushing buttons on a half-broken controller. I ponder about the bad things it's overheard and wonder if that's why it's so broken.

Somehow it still works.

And, I bet, it even enjoys having people to use it.

Maybe it's not so broken.
It has potential.

Maybe I'm not so broken.

Heather
YMCA Oasis Daylight Center

An Ode to Her Rape Whistle

From a black nylon rope around
her neck hangs a silver instrument
bouncing on her tummy as she walks
along. A small ball tassels the dark
inside, waiting to be heard in a different
way…happy.

This whistle, a voice that could not
find its exit from inside. Her defender
lies in waiting.

From a black nylon rope around her
neck, a place of honor, hangs a time
piece that stands still. Recognizing
a day chosen to remember, in blue
plastic it reads, "90 Days Clean."

Her whistle and companion opens
a door to freedom, a silence, attracts
the eyes of many on any given day,
in place.

Robin
Skagit Valley Recovery Community

After Pablo Neruda, "Ode to My Socks"

An Ode to My Glasses

You are the most underappreciated and appreciated object I've ever put on my body. I throw you around before I sleep. I can only imagine how you feel. So—shout out to you for putting up with my ungratefulness and making my vision not look like an unfocused camera lens.

Adriana
YMCA Oasis Daylight Center

After Robin, "Ode to Her Rape Whistle"

I Have Dreams

I have dreams.
In the future, I will help my parents.
Not all my dreams are for myself, but for my family as well. I want to show my parents that it was worth waking up early to go to school.

Ana
Migrant Leaders Club

After Juan Felipe Herrera and Langston Hughes

I Am Waiting

I am waiting for my time to end,
Waiting for the day I get to walk the streets again
Back with the homies, or are they really my homies?
I am waiting to find out,
waiting to see who's real and who's fake.
I am waiting to smell fresh air again
And back in my actual bedroom
Not in a cell with concrete walls and locked doors, with a window you can't even see out of.
I am waiting to look my mother in the eye and say I love you
Without a bullet-proof glass between us.
I am waiting to press restart
Without holding back…
The more I wait the more I think…

Anonymous
Skagit County Juvenile Detention

After Lawrence Ferlinghetti, "I Am Waiting"

Home

Love: Growing up, at a young age, I loved home and all things it had to offer, and my mother saying, I love you deedle bug.

Hate: I hated being the youngest, the sponge of all the dysfunction throughout the family, too young to defend myself from the misery that lurked, my sister with the revenge look in her eyes saying, watch what happens, I'm gonna be watching you while mom's gone. Hating the dread that awaited me.

Fear: Fearing that I may never have a home again, fear of the broken home I once lived in. They say home is where the heart is, but I fear that I'm there, but my heart is never there to be found.

Future: I envision me, home, my own home, my domain, where there is more than enough love to go around. Come one come all, come big and small, my home is the place to be.

Cristian
Skagit County Juvenile Detention

After Alexie

This poem was part of *FilmVerse,* a collaborative project between Underground Writing and Voices of the Children, which used writings from Skagit County Juvenile Detention as the inspiration for short films directed by Mount Vernon High School students. The short film for this poem is available for viewing on the Underground Writing website.

Things Are Arising in Me

Rising to the surface
Like a pimple waiting to pop
Infection to the surface
A pot full of noodles
Bring to a boil
Too hard to eat
Too soft to throw away
The dumpster so full
Nobody caring to take it out
Worth it? Yes.
To everybody else, No
Clean tomorrow they agree
Too late I say
Sunday morning still there
Dirty, foul, infection still there
Until Monday I near the dumpsters
They run to take it out
Already gone
Free
Clean
A new start

Ashley
Skagit County Community Justice Center

After Matthew Siegel, "Sometimes I don't know if I'm having a feeling"

I Celebrate Myself

I celebrate myself like the Psalms of David celebrate God. I celebrate the victories in my life, even my miserable defects. I celebrate the knowledge I've gained from my fallout. I celebrate the good the bad and even the ugly within me. I celebrate the changes that made me stronger. I celebrate myself like I'm the eighth wonder of the world.

Cristian
Skagit County Juvenile Detention

After Walt Whitman, "Song of Myself"

Reflections

The following micro essays were written by Underground Writing's Teaching Writers. To learn more about them and their work, please visit www.undergroundwriting.org

My Dear You

Every Wednesday, two facilitators from Underground Writing stand outside juvenile detention and wait for the heavy metal door to open. We pass the offices on the ground floor and proceed upstairs to another steel door, and another, and finally through a third metal door into the juvie classroom.

Though we usually come in pairs, today I'm alone. The guards are friendly, glad for outside programs that inspire kids. Perhaps they're hopeful we'll come with something that will turn kids around, make them write positive thoughts, make them reflect on the mistakes they've made.

What I love about Underground Writing is that it's not about any of these things. I'm here with good literature in tow, to explore along with the kids. To see, through reading and writing, what arises in me. To see what speaks to them. To hear their voices and share mine. We're in it together, wherever it may lead.

I'd read a story in *Tin House Magazine* that stayed with me long after reading it. I don't normally bring fiction to juvie—full stories are too lengthy for our limited time together. We don't want this to feel like a test of reading ability. We want to ruminate on the images. We want the words to connect on a deeper level. For that reason, we often bring poetry. But I wondered what would happen if I brought only the beginning of the story. Leaving it open-ended might create more room for us to imagine and reflect. To see ourselves within the narrative.

Three kids are escorted in by the guards. Two teen boys and a girl enter as they've been taught, walking with hands clasped behind them, single file. They sit at the table in bright orange pants and sweatshirts, feet in plastic sandals. They put their Underground Writing notebooks before them. The guard hands out golf pencils and takes a seat near the table to watch.

We start, as always, with freewriting. We're instructed to tell them: no profanity allowed, no gang references. We call this exercise the brain spill—our chance to simply purge ourselves of the day's thoughts. The kids scribble away and put down their pencils. "Anyone want to share?" I ask. No one does.

We move on to the story I've brought, a piece by Rachel Khong entitled, "My Dear You." A person has gone to heaven. We're not sure if it's male or female—even better. We can imagine ourselves here. The person tells us that if you die in a manner that destroys your face, you get to choose a new one. The kids are intrigued. We read on.

A guy named Richard meets the new arrival. He's like a prison guard. Turns out the narrator got dragged under the water by a crocodile—hence the need for a new face. S/he wonders what the new face is for. Would there be eating in heaven? Tanning? Was there a possibility of falling in love again? Yes, Richard says. All of the above. Then David Bowie rides by on a bicycle. But it might not have been David Bowie. It could just be someone who chose his face.

What are some of your questions about the piece? I ask.

They want to know if there are guards in heaven. They want to know how old the person is. They want to know male or female. The boys think female. The girl thinks male. We laugh about David Bowie. They want to know if that's really what happens in heaven. They wish I'd brought the rest of the story.

I fill in a little more: The person goes over to a computer to pick new features. The character doesn't want to be Chinese anymore. S/he presses a button at random. Ends up Chinese.

We talk about what we'd change about ourselves if given the chance. I'm careful not to imply that they're flawed, in need of a retrofit. But I'm curious—if given the chance, would they change anything? Would I?

We move to writing. I prime the pump by suggesting they start with the line, "If I had a do-over." They begin. The boys keep going and going. The girl finishes quickly, putting down her pencil and looking around the room. After a few minutes, I ask if anyone would like to share.

If I had a do-over, one of the boys begins, I wouldn't make my mom so sad. I would stay true to myself. I wouldn't go along with what everyone told me to do. The guard nods.
The girl reads: I wouldn't change much ...or I wouldn't recognize myself.

This one surprises me more. The kids are used to writing what they think we want to hear. But she has a rare confidence. Despite all that's happened, she still wants to be herself.

We end with a poem by Chloe Honum and create a poem of our own—a list of things remembered from childhood. When I return home, another poem by Honum catches my eye. It's called "Teaching Poetry at the Juvenile Detention Center in Fayetteville, Arkansas":

> It's cold and the light is blurry,
> the fluorescents spasming,
>
> the walls a steely gray.
> Each child is given a pencil.
>
> Their cells are just beyond
> the heavy sliding doors.
> They write get-away poems
> and treehouse poems.
>
> Sack of weed and siren poems.
>
> A flea appears on my arm and
> quivers, like a fleck of onyx.
>
> I watch it bite and gleam and the boys sitting across from
> me watch it, too. In a cement
>
> tomb, hope is anything
> that travels in big leaps.*

A. Muia
Teaching Writer | Fiction

---

* Chloe Honum, "Teaching Poetry at the Juvenile Detention Center in Fayetteville, Arkansas, " from *Then Winter* (2017), Bull City Press.

Voices Underground

We read a poem by Li Young-Lee, "Little Father," and in response a fifteen-year-old boy in Juvenile Detention wrote about the time his dad ran over him with a car.

> It took him a second to realize
> what happened but he said that
> he told me to get out of the way
> at least my bike was OK

This was last summer. It stuck with me.

Last month this same teenager walked into our Underground Writing group in the classroom. (Over time, you see youth return, again and again, to this place.) I put him on the spot by saying I still remembered something he wrote a year before.

"Yeah?" Yeah, I told him. Did he remember what it was? He did; he summarized the memory.

I asked him—for the audience of five other teenagers sitting around the two round tables in their bright orange sweats, listening—why he thought I remembered it. He shook his head, eyebrows up, honestly not sure why that lousy memory would stick with the writing teacher. "Cuz it's f--, uh, messed up?"

Yeah, I said. But more basic than that: he wrote it down, I said, plain, simple, no flowery words. The event spoke for itself. I hoped this would dispel other students' fears of writing being about getting fancy with our words.

"And because you dared to read it out loud. You shared it with us. Otherwise I wouldn't have heard that story, or your powerful voice."

His face was blank. So what.

These youth are used to their voices not being heard or wanted. They are accustomed to not being seen.

We were not discussing metaphor that day. But I am now.

Unless we the adults behind the wheel of our communities hear these stories, hear the voices of young lives being caught under the gears of our courts and legal systems, we won't know we need to hit the brakes. Or sober up.

In the last year, four of the boys—all between fourteen and sixteen years old—in our Juvenile Detention workshops have been charged as adults in the courtroom across the street. They each face over a decade in adult prison. None of them are white.

I can imagine where they are headed. Because, as an adult prison and gang chaplain, I've also been writing letters to a twenty-one-year-old in a solitary confinement cell across Washington state. He was already one of the highest violent inmates in the system when I met him. He'd stabbed multiple guards in the face, neck, when they entered his cell. The homies called him Lil' Saint. Saint was sentenced, age fifteen, as an adult.

But in our letters, I was curious about him. He told me horror stories. Being whipped as a child, locked in the bathroom for days. Through writing, he made the connection between his childhood treatment and current "animal" rage, lashing out, at being caged. He used his pen, his voice. He was heard, and he had compassion on himself. He's now reading Steinbeck, ancient Roman histories, and has earned his way off of high security levels.

He never wrote a poem. But his writing I'm most proud of was the letter he wrote our county prosecutor, at our gentle request. He told his story on behalf of a kid in Juvenile Detention he's never met. He raised his voice so that the man behind the legal wheel in our county might, hopefully, hit the brakes—and see a child about to be crushed underground.

The prosecutor still has not lowered the charges. I'm not even sure if he read Saint's prison-envelope letter. It's likely he'll never hear Saint's voice.

Do we?

Chris Hoke
Teaching Writer | Non-Fiction

White Walls

"How do you say his name?" they ask me.

"*Xu* is pronounced like shoe," I tell them, oversimplifying the Mandarin pronunciation: "It's like what you're wearing on your feet."

Then I catch myself. My students at the juvenile facility don't wear shoes, but booties, along with their orange jumpsuits and hands they must cross behind their backs when they move. Though it's an easy mistake to make, thinking of us as just people together, one (me) older. In spite of all that dehumanizes them, my group is defiantly human.

Many, though not all, of my students belong to gangs, something that was also true of several of my cousins. I mention this fact in class one day, but they look at me blankly. I am older, I teach, I don't wear a jumpsuit; in their eyes I come from a different world.

Today I have brought to them poems from a Chinese poet, Xu Lizhi, who worked at the infamous FoxConn sweatshop in China for fourteen hours a day making electronics, slept packed in a dorm with other workers, got paid little, and had no ability to leave. Xu killed himself at twenty-four, which I do not mention to my students.

Xu and poets like him wrote poems of confinement and despair, sending them out on cell phones, their chief means of communication with the outside world. I had no idea how my group, many held by forces outside themselves in confined social groups, would react to a poem from such a distant culture.

"I swallowed an iron moon," Xu wrote of his forced labor. I ask my students what they have had to swallow. C., whip smart, charming, mischievous in person, but dead serious when he writes, describes swallowing a life that feels stalled, empty, "staring at white walls hours on end." He felt deeply everything Xu was describing. These two young men, Xu and C., did indeed cross half the world and speak to one another. If people read his poem, C. told me, they would know something important about him, as he now knew something of the soul of Xu Lizhi.

I often read student poems full of helplessness and despair. I praise and honor these, but often ask them to "flip the script": imagine yourself five years from now; who would you be if you became what you wanted, if you didn't have to swallow anymore? It's surprising how much time it can take my students to imagine that possibility. Will writing about it cause them all to become that person? No, but it might help. And at least for a little while, as we read aloud together, we honor that bit of light inside of us.

Susanne Paola Antonetta
Teaching Writer | Poetry and Non-Fiction

Together in the Game

In August, we held our second Underground Writing Intensive in Skagit County Juvenile Detention. That week, team members held daily workshops focused on Jason Reynolds' award-winning novel in verse *Long Way Down*. The book's dedication reads, "For all the young brothers and sisters in detention centers around the country, the ones I've seen and the ones I haven't. You are loved." It was a powerful week filled with moving moments as the students devoured the book and responded by writing poems, dialogues, memories, and letters to the author.

To set the intensive slightly apart from our other workshops, we held it in the morning instead of the afternoon. On the second day, I noticed all three of the guys walked in holding decks of cards, as they had done the day before.

"What's with the cards?"

"We just had rec," one student explained. "We play."

"Yeah?" I was intrigued.

The guys usually walk in empty handed, their hands clasped behind their backs as instructed until they are given their notebooks and pencils.

"What do you play?"

They looked at each other. "Spades. Oh, Gee. Stuff like that."

The moment didn't seem like a big one, but it made me think of a passage from another novel by Jason Reynolds, *The Boy in the Black Suit.* When I went back for a regular weekly workshop a few weeks later, I brought that excerpt and a Calvin Forbes poem titled "The Card Players."

After telling them I picked the pieces for the day based on that moment the month before, we warmed up by reading the Forbes poem. We talked about metaphor, how the poet seemed to be writing about something simple—sitting in on a card game with his three older brothers—but how much more there was there on the page.

"I like this part," J. said.

*The three of them (ace king and a wild card)**

We talked about metaphor. About games. And then we wrote a little about playing cards. The writing wasn't as earth shattering or arresting as it sometimes is, but it felt comfortable. Like sitting down to a hand of spades with friends.

We then read the excerpt from Reynolds' book. In the story, the main character, Matt, is simultaneously grieving his mother's death, dealing with his father's relapse into alcohol, and trying to keep his life straight. Mr. Ray, the director of the funeral parlor in the neighborhood, starts looking out for him. Early in the book, Mr. Ray scoffs at how chess is elevated by the park players and folks in their Brooklyn neighborhood.

---

* Calvin Forbes, "The Card Players" from *Poetry* (2016), available at https://www.poetryfoundation.org/poetrymagazine/poems/90669/the-card-players-57d18c33f371c

*It's an overrated game that people, especially New Yorkers, think is the friggin' holy grail of games. Like you can learn all there is to know about life by playing chess. A bunch of bull.**

The guys laughed at this part, but we kept reading. Mr. Ray then challenges Matt to a game of War. As they flip the cards, trading hands, Mr. Ray explains that this is really the game of life.

Sometimes I win. And sometimes I lose. And sometimes," he continued while flipping another one, "I can lose and lose and lose and I don't know why. But there's nothing I can do but just keep flipping the cards. Eventually I'll win again. As long as you got cards to keep turning, you're fine. Now that's life," he said, pushing another hand I won over to me.

"That's pretty good," a guard sitting in on our workshop said after we finished reading.

The guys agreed.

And then we wrote. We wrote about what we each thought was the game of life, thinking about metaphor, about the parallels between the simple and the complex.

D. disagreed with Mr. Ray in his piece, asserting that chess was the game of life.

---

* Jason Reynolds, *The Boy in the Black Suit* (2016), Atheneum Books for Young Readers.

The streets is kind of like a game of chess. You start out as a pawn...but you want to make the right moves or you could lose the game, where there is no restart."

Our hour passed, and I drove away reflecting on how the writing didn't go as well as I had hoped. But there was something else there, a feeling in the room—a feeling that we were all there together, flipping cards, turning them one by one. I hope that's what we're doing week after week: reminding them and ourselves that none of us is out of cards yet, and every word we read, write, and share builds the deck a little thicker and keeps us in the game a little longer.

Jennifer Bradbury
Teaching Writer | Fiction

Sometimes There's God

We have a tough audience this afternoon at the Migrant Leaders Club at LaVenture Middle School. We have just read the poem "Bent to the Earth," by Blas Manuel De Luna, about a traumatic childhood encounter with Customs and Immigration. The five-year-old narrator watches as immigration officers run their van into an irrigation ditch, threaten the driver with batons, and handcuff his mother.

"What do you think?" Nobody says anything for a long time. Are they bored? Indifferent? Angry? One of the older girls finally breaks the spell.

"You white people just don't get it!"

"Why do you think that is?" More silence, longer this time. The fluorescent lights are buzzing.

"Because it never happens to you."

"I will probably never experience what you've experienced," I say. "What's the next best thing to help me get it?" The classroom goes quiet again, but now most of us are scratching in our notebooks.

Juan writes about a jacket. In the summer, he picks strawberries with his family. In the strawberry fields, the rows are lined with black plastic to stifle the weeds. The pickers go out early in the morning, and it's cold, so Juan wears a black jacket with long sleeves.

By afternoon the sun is beating down on them, and the fields are steamy and radiating heat, but Juan leaves his jacket on all day, so he won't get burned. He even tugs the sleeves down to protect his hands. Juan's words make all of us sweat a little.

During Underground Writing workshops, we always write with our students. Our primary mission, though, is to encourage them to tell their own stories. Accomplishing that goal, I have discovered, requires a truce with silence.

For those of us who are both writers and teaching writers, tension hums as relentlessly as the overhead lights—the temptation to fill the silence with words. Writers are all about filling empty spaces. Silence is intimidating in the same way the cursor blinking on a blank screen is intimidating: it demands something from us. We feel compelled to respond not only (or even mostly) because we have something to *say*; we respond because we want to know that we are *heard*.

Maybe silence is intimidating because we wonder whether anybody is listening. Maybe that's what the kids in the workshop wonder, too.

Their silence demands a certain kind of listening—deeply empathetic and respectful of the guts it takes to reveal our inner selves. In the theatre, playwrights craft silences like these, and they are often the most revealing moments on stage. In Tennessee William's *A Streetcar Named Desire*, for example, about halfway through the play, Blanche thinks she might finally have found a savior in Mitch:
"You need somebody. And I need somebody, too. Could it be—you and me, Blanche?" After a pause, Blanche ends the scene:

"Sometimes—there's God—so quickly."

There is silence all around that line, wordless space in which we absorb everything that Blanche cannot bring herself to say, and her fragile hopes resonate with our own. Not unlike a prayer.

There is a similar moment in Samuel Beckett's *Waiting for Godot.* In that play two tramps meet every day under a bare tree. They are waiting for a mysterious figure who never comes, and while they wait, they mock the futility of their lives in a relentless patter of dialogue.

When the curtain rises on Act 2, the next day, the tree inexplicably has leaves. The script calls for a long pause while everyone considers the tree. In the silence, we all become aware of an unseen presence who might be watching, listening, and (dare we hope) prepared to intervene.

Maybe it's just the humming of the overhead lights, but during the workshops at the Migrant Leaders Club, I have begun to think of the silence as a sentient being. It insists that we meet on common ground, where it doesn't matter so much that we are brown or white, documented or undocumented, English- or Spanish-speaking. Only then do the words come.

People who are impossibly far away, and sometimes no longer alive, walk into the room and join us. The dad deported to Mexico when his daughter was a baby. A woman with pricked fingers and red-stained hands after another day of picking raspberries. The man who chased you out of your own neighborhood on Halloween, yelling, "Go back where you came from."

It turns out we don't have an audience at the Migrant Leaders Club. We *are* the audience. Our role is to make space for silence and pay attention to whatever arises out of it, in whatever language.

To resent the warmth of a sunny afternoon with a kid who has never enjoyed a summer break. To feel the terror of a child watching as his mother is handcuffed by men with batons.

To sit quietly, as poet William Carlos Williams puts it,

> with long lapses of silence
> … aware of the stream
> that has no language, coursing
> beneath the quiet heaven of
> your eyes[1*]

Jennifer Morison Hendrix
Teaching Writer | Playwriting and Non-fiction

---

* William Carlos Williams, *Paterson* (1963), New York: New Direction.

The Restorative Word

J., a local youth, was booked in Juvenile Detention on July 8, 2015, the day of our first ever Underground Writing workshop. In November, J. and I began to meet regularly on Mondays for an hour. Inside a locked 8-by-6 room, with security cameras and heavy doors, J. began to share about his upbringing in a middle-class home, the conflicts that began to tear his parents apart, and the present-day entrenched isolation within his immediate family. This familial decline led to a spiraling sense of self, and subsequently assisted J.'s descent into depression, drugs, and criminal offenses.

Unable to discuss the details of his case (per his lawyer's advice), we conversed around and near the subject. And J. continued to attend Underground Writing workshops.

Feedback from J.'s public defender was extremely encouraging for our program early on: after beginning to regularly read and write, J.'s whole outlook changed. In fact, it helped him get off antidepressants. And J. was indeed excited about writing. We talked a great deal about fiction and poetry. (He enjoys reading Sherman Alexie and Steinbeck, Sylvia Plath and Emily Dickinson and Jimmy Santiago Baca.) We looked over and edited his many short stories in progress. One day, almost like a confession, he told me he'd written his first poem. Youth are not allowed pencils in their cells…J. told me he'd written the poem in soap on his mirror.

This image has stayed with me for over a year. I can picture the scene in which J. has just completed his poem. I see him, in his orange jumpsuit, gazing into the mirror at the reflection he has so often been terrified of, angry with, and ashamed of:

himself. But this time he's seeing himself with words striped across his body. Unlike the black vertical bars of a cell, these are white and horizontal, words appearing almost as stabilizing bars that he can grasp. As he gazes at the lines, proud of the poem he has created, J. sees himself embodied in and through words, a revision in progress, a version of what could be.

* * *

Some of the student writing that I've read over the past year—including J.'s—suggests an inability for students to picture a better future, sometimes any future at all. They feel stuck in the present moment. Underground Writing aims to facilitate encounters with good literature and to provide generative writing prompts that allow students to re-view their lives. We hope to assist in the restoration of each student's imagination.

"What does this image remind you of?" I ask, holding up a piece of paper for the students to view during a workshop in Juvenile Detention.

J. smirks and looks across the across the table at Diana and Mary.

"Bars," he says. "Right? Prison bars."

"Yeah, prison bars," D. says. M. nods in agreement.

We talk about living in a cell. The youth—ages 15 to 16—describe it as "a dark hole, a pit, a—"

"That's vivid," I say. "Hold up, though, because I want you to write some of this down."

I hand out "The Face of a Cell," a poem written by a youth in Seattle's juvenile detention system. We each take a turn reading— "If my cell were a person…" it begins.

The first writing prompt: write a physical description of your cell. The results are varied: "I'm behind the red metal door …locked until the guards unlock it …staring at the off-white colored walls, off-white color floors…I realize if I don't stop running, I will keep ending up behind the red metal door."

I transition the group. "Sometimes we need to see in a different way, to have our vision altered—right?"

J. furrows his eyebrows and tosses his head slightly back. "What?"

I pull out a piece of paper. "What do these remind you of?"

After a pause, "Lines, or like the bars turned sideways," D. says.

"Right," I say. "Now watch this."

Out from behind the image, I slide a paper with a Reginald Dwayne Betts' poem in couplets that mirror the horizontal bars.

"Whoa," J. says, leaning forward. D. and M. smile and gaze at the image.

"This is a poem in couplets, or what rappers might call 'bars'. When we view things differently—say, hard situations like being inside Juvenile Detention—they can start to become something else. And we can do that sort of thing through writing."

Our second writing prompt: revisit your cell in your mind and write about the feelings and thoughts you have there.

The students read the results from their notebooks: "I think about gettin' out… Sometimes I feel no one pays attention to what I want…I think that I don't belong here."

"Let's transition to another scene," I say, handing out Czeslaw Milosz' poem, "A Gift." We discuss the narrator's life, the way he's chosen to see things, and his sense of the future. After five minutes on the poem, I show the students a final picture. It's the same as the second image, but with a single dark line on each side of the horizontal bars. There are a few guesses and confused looks.

"It's a ladder," I say. The kids sigh and laugh. "Difficult things can help us see differently, even better."

"Makes sense," M. says.

"For the final prompt, I want you to take the writing you've already done today and climb up it, as it were, so that you can see a future for yourself…and then I want you to write about what you see there."

"…looking at the sky, thinking about myself," J. writes, "…I think I'm a good kid."

M. begins, "I think I can graduate. I always try my best..."

In a fitting conclusion, D. shares last: "I want to climb out of the hole I'm digging myself and see what I can accomplish...I want to see myself getting past all the things I've been through and not let them define me anymore."

Matt Malyon
Teaching Writer and Director | Poetry

Afterword

Resources

Underground Writing facilitates generative encounters with literature spanning the tradition—from ancient texts to those written in our workshops.

Honoring the transforming power of the word, we believe that attentive reading leads to attentive writing, and that attentive writing has the power to assist in the restoration of communities, the imagination, and individual lives.

The following selections of poetry, prose, and drama were used in Underground Writing workshops.

<u>Alexie, Sherman</u>
The Absolutely True Diary of a Part-Time Indian
"After the First Lightening"
"Family Portrait"
"Father Coming Home"
"The Fight or Flight Response"
"Futures"
"Grandmother"
"Indian Boy Love Song (#1)"
"Indian Boy Love Song (#2)"
"Last Will and Testament"
"Marriage"
"That Place Where Ghosts of Salmon Jump"
"The Pow Wow at the End of the World"
"Reservation Blues"
"Superman and Me"
"When I Die"

<u>Akhmatova, Anna</u>
"Over the snowdrift's hard crust ..." from *Requiem* (Hemschemeyer, trans.)

<u>Alarcón, Francisco X.</u>
"Ode to My Shoes"

<u>Amichai, Yehuda</u>
"I came back once more" (Abramson, Parfitt, trans.)

Andrade, Jorge Carrera
"The Guest" (Lee and Martin, trans.)

Angelou, Maya
"Caged Bird"
"Still I Rise"

Anonymous (Free Verse – Montana)
"Where I'm From"

Anonymous (Pongo Writing)
"The New Park"

Anonymous Youth (InsideOUT Writers)
"Give More: InsideOUT Writers Speak"

Antonetta, Susanne Paola
"Columbines"

Baca, Jimmy Santiago
"2"
"33"
"A Daily Joy To Be Alive"
A Place to Stand
"Cloudy Day"
"I Am Offering You This Poem"
"Letters Come From Prison"
"Old Man"
"Oppression"
"Praise"
"What Is Broken Is What God Blesses"

Barnhart, Graham
"Notice and Focus Exercise"

Basho
Haiku "151–162"

Belli, Carlos Germán
"Tortilla" (Gil-Montero, trans.)

Berry, Wendell
"The Peace of Wild Things"

Betts, Reginald Dwayne
"Love in the Time of Chain-link Fences"
"Prison"
"Red Onion State Prison"
"Shahid Reads His Own Palm"
"Tell This to the People You Love"

Biele, Joelle
"Paradise Lost"

Blackmore, Janice, ed.
Dream Fields: A Peek into the World of Migrant Youth (2012)

Borowicz, Karina
"Escape"

Bradbury, Jennifer
Outside In

Brautigan, Richard
"It's Raining in Love"
"Your Catfish Friend"

Brooks, Gwendolyn
"Sadie and Maud"
"We Real Cool"
"The Pool Players: Seven at the Golden Shovel"

Broumas, Olga
"Cinderella"

Bukowski, Charles
"born to lose"
"this moment"

C (Skagit County Juvenile Detention)
"I Was a Girl"

C.S. (Whatcom Juvenile Justice Project)
"Character"

Carey (Pongo Writing)
"Good Day | Bad Day"

Carroll, Lewis
"Jabberwocky"

Cedering, Siv
"Hands"

Celia (Migrant Leaders Club)
"My Life is Difficult"

Chang, Victoria
"Is It Rude To Tell Men That You Don't"

Chbosky, Stephen
Perks of Being a Wallflower

Chihuailaf, Elikura
"I Still Want to Dream in this Valley" (Bierhorst, trans.)

Childress, Susanna
"It's the First Thing"

Cilviana (Migrant Leaders Club)
"Estoy Aqui!" (Here I Am!)

Cohen, Leonard
"Steer Your Way"

Collins, Billy
"Introduction to Poetry"

Courtenay, Bryce
The Power of One

Crane, Stephen
"War is Kind"

D., Chuck (Public Enemy)
"Fight the Power"

Dante
The Divine Comedy (Mandelbaum, trans.)

Darwish, Mahmoud
"And We Love Life" (Joudah, trans.)
"I Belong There"
"On the Earth" (Akash/Forché, trans.)
"Remainder of Life" (Joudah, trans.)

Davis (Pongo Writing)
"How Do I Start a New Beginning"

De Luna, Blas Manuel
"Bent to the Earth"

Denon (InsideOUT Writers)
"The Risen Sun to the Sky"

Destery (YMCA Oasis Daylight Center)
"Dear Dad"

Destiny (InsideOUT Writers)
"The Things I'll Never Tell You"

Diaz,Natalie
"If Eve Side-Stealer & Mary Busted-Chest Ruled the World"
"It Was the Animals"

Dickinson, Emily
"I died for beauty, but was scarce"
"This is my letter to the world"

Dillard, Annie
"God in the Doorway"

Dostoevsky, Fyodor
A Writer's Diary

Dove, Rita
"Heart to Heart"

Duncan, David James
"The Mickey Mantle Koan"

Duritz, Adam (Counting Crows)
"Omaha"

Dylan, Bob
"Blowin' in the Wind"
"It's Alright Ma (I'm Only Bleeding)"
"Percy's Song"
"The Times They Are A-Changin'"

Dylan, Jakob
"War is Kind"

Eber (Migrant Leaders Club)
"Struggling to Survive"

E.R. (Whatcom Juvenile Justice Project)
"10 Things I'm Afraid of"

Erdrich, Louise
"The Red Convertible"

Espada, Martín
Alabanza

Faiz, Faiz Ahmed
"Before You Came" (Lazard, trans.)

Falkoff, Marc, ed.
Poems from Guantánamo: The Detainees Speak

Ferlinghetti, Lawrence
"I Am Waiting"

Forché, Carolyn
"The Colonel"
"The Visitor"

Ford, Katie
"Foreign Song"

Foster, R. Daniel
"Bad Luck Meditation"

Frost, Robert
"The Road Not Taken"

Fuertes, Gloria
"Prayer" (Barker, trans.)

G., Rafael
"Hanging On by a Thin String"

Gay, Ross
"becoming a horse"

Ginsberg, Allen
"My Sad Self"

Gioia, Dana
"Too Bad"

Guevarra, Ernesto Ché
Motorcycle Diaries

Guthrie, Woody
"This Land Is Your Land"

Hayden, Robert
"Those Winter Sundays"

Hayes, Terrance
"Barberism"

Heather (YMCA Oasis Daylight Center)
"Potential"

Hendrix, Jennifer Morison
The Hungry Season

Herrera, Juan Felipe
"Hard Hooks That Fold You Down To Your Knees"
"Hey, Phil"
"Los Angeles"

Hinton, S. E.
The Outsiders

Hirsch, Edward
"Wild Gratitude"

Hoke, Chris
Wanted

Homer
The Odyssey (Lattimore, trans.)

Honum, Chloe
"Before Group Meditation in the Psychiatric Ward"

Hudgins, Andrew
"Fist"

Hughes, Langston
"Dreams"
"Dream Variations"
"Fulfillment"
"I Dream a World"
"I, Too, Sing America"
"Mother to Son"
"Song for Billie Holiday"
"Theme for English B"
"To You"

Ignatow, David
"The Bagel"

Janet (Migrant Leaders Club)
"You See Me As Trouble"

Janice (Skagit Valley Recovery Community)
"Trying to catch up with you"

Jarman, Mark
"Through the Waves"

Jeremy (Pongo Writing)
"The Face of a Cell"

Jess, Tyehimba
"My Name is Sissiretta Jones"

JN (WritersCorps)
"America's Beauty Gone"

Johnson, Kimberly
"On Divination by Knuckle Bones"
"Vigil"

Josiah (Pongo Writing)
"Quiet in the Room, Loud in Your Head"

Juan (Migrant Leaders Club)
"I Am a Field Worker and I Am Tired

Julio (Migrant Leaders Club)
"The Promised Land"

Kamieńska, Anna
"A Talk With Mother"
"At the Border of Paradise"
"Gratitude"
"The Lamp"
"Transformation" (Curzon and Drabik, trans.)

Kaminsky, Ilya
"Dancing in Odessa"

Kawanza (InsideOUT Writers)
"The New Me"

Khong, Rachel
"My Dear You"

Kim, Suji Kwock
"Skins"

Kincaid, Jamaica
"Girl"
"The Letter from Home"
A Small Place

King Jr., Martin Luther
"I Have A Dream"

Knight, Etheridge
"A Poem for Myself (or Blues for a Mississippi Black Boy)

Komunyakaa, Yusef
"Facing It"

Kraushaar, Mark
"I Died and Went to Heaven"

Lee, Li-Young
"Little Father"

Levertov, Denise
"The Avowal"
"The Secret"
"Weeping Woman"

Limón, Ada
"A New National Anthem"

Lizhi, Xu (sweatshop laborer)
Poems sent via text message

Logan (Skagit County Juvenile Detention)
"Dear America"

Lorca, Federico Garcia
"The Little Mute Boy"

Malyon, Matt
"Family Photo"
"Icarus Ashore"
"Soundings"

Mandelstam, Osip
"And I Was Alive"
"Hard Night"
"Night Piece" (Wiman, trans.)

Marcela (Migrant Leaders Club)
"Dear America"

M., Arturo (InsideOUT Writers)
"The first thing that makes me happy. . ."

Masters, Edgar Lee
Spoon River Anthology

McCrae, Shane
"Claiming Language"

Mendoza, Jasmyne
"Go Inside a Beating Heart" (Writers in the Schools, Seattle)

Miłosz, Czesław
"A Gift"

Momaday, N. Scott
House Made of Dawn

Montale, Eugenio
"In the Smoke" (Singh, trans.)

Moord, M. (*Iron City Magazine*, No. 1)
"What If"

Morgenstern, Erin
The Night Circus

Morales, Miguel M
"This is a Migrant Poem"

Mueller, Melinda
"Monument Valley, Full Moon"

Muia, A.
"The Vermilion Saint"

Neruda, Pablo
"We Have Lost Even"

Nye, Naomi Shihab
"Rain"

O'Brien, Tim
The Things They Carried

Orr, Gregory
The Blessing

Parker, Robin (Skagit Valley Recovery Community)
"Ode to Her Rape Whistle"

Pavese, Cesare
"Words from Confinement" (Arrowsmith, trans.)

Pea, Vika
"I Wonder"

Petty, Tom
"I Won't Back Down"
"Wildflowers"

PM (WritersCorps)
"Love Poem to Love"

Prado, Adélia
"The Alphabet in the Park"
"Meditation of the Kings Among His Troops" (Watson, trans.)

Reagler, Robin
"The Way"

Rich, Adrienne
"Write as if your life depended on it"

Rilke, Rainer Maria
"Letter 1" from *Letters to a Young Poet* (Stephen Mitchell, trans.)
"The hour is striking so close above me" from *Book of Hours* (Barrows and Macy, trans.)

R., Michael (Write Around Portland)
"The Heart of the Lotus"

Rottet, Robert
"Into the Sun"
"Over There"
"Reverb"
"When She Speaks"

S., David (InsideOUT Writers)
"Let emotions flow then let them go …"

Sappho
"Poem Fragments 54–60" (Barnard, trans.)

Sassoon, Siegfried
"Everyone Sang"

Schwertfeger, Robert (Skagit County Juvenile Detention)
"Dear System"

Sean (Pongo Writing)
"How I'm Feeling"

Serpas, Martha
"Lying in the Middle of the Field"

Sexton, Anne
"Lullaby"

Shakur, Tupac
"The Rose That Grew from Concrete"

Shaw, Luci
"The Slow Pleasures"

Shaw, Robert
"In the Rear-View Mirror"

Shelton, Richard
"The Stones"

Shy, Shoshauna
"Bringing My Son to the Police Station to Be Fingerprinted"

Siegel, Matthew
"Sometimes I don't know if I'm having a feeling"

Sigurðsson, Magnús
"Dark Forest"

Skoog, Ed
"Gwendolyn Brooks Park, Topeka"

Smith, Betty
A Tree Grows in Brooklyn

Södergran, Edith
The Trees of My Childhood" (Mörling and Ellerström, trans.)

Solie, Karen
"Untitled"
"X"

Sophia (Skagit County Juvenile Detention)
"Thinking"

Soto, Gary
"Field"
"Mission Tire Factory"
"Oranges"

ST (WritersCorps)
"Memory"

Stănescu, Nichita
"In Praise of People" (Cotter, trans.)

Stafford, William
"A Catechism"
"Scars"

Steinbeck, John
The Pastures of Heaven

Suk, Julie
"Loving the Hands"

Szybist, Mary
"Here, There Are Blueberries"

Szymborska, Wisława
"Miracle Fair"

Teresa (Migrant Leaders Club)
"*La Mata*-Chickens"

Thomas, Dylan
"Do Not Go Gentle into That Good Night"

Thomas, R.S.
"The Flower"

Tranströmer, Tomas
"Nine Haiku from Hällby Young Offenders' Prison"
"Tracks"

Tsvetaeva, Marina
"A kiss on the forehead" from *Poems for Blok* (Kaminsky and Valentine, trans.)

Valdés, Olvido García
"I am hauling things like an old village . . ."
"What Do You Expect, Heart?"

Valery, Paul
"The Angel Handed Me a Book"

Verónica (Migrant Leaders Club)
"Crossing the Border"

Verónica and Carolina (Migrant Leaders Club)
"We Are All Humans"

Victor (Skagit County Juvenile Detention)
"Dear America"

Victoriyah (InsideOUT Writers)
"A Second Look"

Vilariño, Idea
"Almost Every Time" (Kercheval, trans.)
"Metamorphosis" (Fainlight, trans.)

Vollmer, Matthew
"The Subordinate Fragment"

Walcott, Derek
Omeros

Whitman, Walt
"I Hear America Singing"
"Song of Myself"

Williams, William Carlos
"Iris"
"This Is Just To Say"
Paterson

Woodson, Jacqueline
Locomotion

Wright, Charles
"Like the New Moon, My Mother Drifts Through the Night Sky"

Wright, Franz
"Goodbye"

Wright, James
"A Blessing"

Wrigley, Robert
"After a Rainstorm"

Xavier (Pongo Writing)
"If God Were Looking at My Life"

Xu, Lizhi
"Iron Moon"

Yesica (Migrant Leaders Club)
"Choices"

Zagajewski, Adam
"A Star"
"Ordinary Life"
"Poetry Searches for Radiance"
"Try To Praise the Mutilated World" (Cavanagh, trans.)

Zamora, Javier
"The Pier of La Herradura"
"Saguaros"

Notes

What Is a Teaching Writer?

In addition to their work with Underground Writing, our Teaching Writers are actively writing, publishing, and teaching. In our program, they facilitate creative writing workshops and write alongside our students. They model and discuss both the in-process nature of creating poetry and prose inside our workshops, and the life of a working writer outside them.

A Dialogic Literary Convention

The attribution *"After..."* used throughout *What No One Ever Tells You* honors the influence of a previously read piece of literature. This influence shows itself in a variety of ways in students' work—the line used to start a new piece of writing, allusions to another piece of literature, or an imitation of style or mood or content.

Use of this convention in our anthology evidences our love of the whole tradition of literature, from—as we tell our students—ancient texts to those written in our workshops. It also reflects one of our fundamental beliefs: in taking up a pencil and moving it across the page to form letters, which become words, which become lines, we circumnavigate the things that so often separate us, and we become—famous or not—part of the unceasing river of literature.

Next Steps

If this anthology creates a desire in you to do similar work, consider taking your next step by connecting with *One Year Writing in the Margins.*

This initiative challenges Teaching Writers to spend one year facilitating creative writing workshops outside the academy, in at-risk communities, where the transforming powers of reading and writing can be a matter of life and death.

www.oneyearwritinginthemargins.org

Acknowledgements

Thank you to the editors of the following publications, where pieces in this anthology have appeared, sometimes in earlier versions: the *Bellingham Review, Iron City Magazine,* and the YMCA Oasis Daylight Center's Fall 2017 and Fall 2018 *Zines.*

Thanks to the Washington State Arts Commission (ArtsWA) for the grant that helped us publish this book. Thanks, in particular, to Miguel Guillen and Hannah Dahlke.

Thanks to our inaugural Board: Armando Ruiz, Brian Paxton, Isela Martinez-Shouse, and Matt Malyon.

Thanks to our Site Hosts: Shawn Thompson, Skagit County Juvenile Detention; Janice Blackmore, Migrant Leaders Club (Mount Vernon School District); Randi Breuer and Justin Krupa, YMCA Oasis Daylight Center; Elizabeth Morgan, Brigid Collins; and Deputy Mark Rinas, Sgt. Polly Storie, Sgt. Aaron McIntosh, Lt. Deanna Randall-Secrest, and Chief Don Marlowe, Skagit County Community Justice Center.

Thanks to our Advisory Board: Claudia Avendano-Ibarra, Jimmy Santiago Baca, Josh Banner, Janice Blackmore, Susanna Childress, Josh Cook, Annie Day, Elizabett (Liz) Eslinger, Bruce Herman, Quiara Alegría Hudes, Janice Jackson, Sgt. Aaron McIntosh, Molly McNulty, Laurie Parker, Kathy Prunty, Robin Reagler, Robert Schwertfeger, Lt. Deanna Randall-Secrest, Luci Shaw, Karen Solie, Amy Swauger, Danna Thompson, Shawn Thompson, Natalie Volin, Cornelia "Corri" Wells, Loren and Mary Ruth Wilkinson, and Jimmy Wu.

Thanks to our Community Collaborators: Brigid Collins, Christ Episcopal Church, Easton's Books, Lincoln Theater, Migrant Leaders Club (Mount Vernon School District), MoNA - Museum of Northwest Art, Red Door Thrift Store, Skagit County Community Justice Center, Skagit County Juvenile Detention, Skagit River Poetry Foundation, Skagit Valley College's Community Integration Project, Underground Ministries, Village Books, and YMCA Oasis Daylight Center.

Thanks to Paul Hanson, Candee Blanc, and Kelli Terpsma of Village Books, Bellingham, WA. Thanks also to Brendan Clark for first version help. Thanks to David Cornelius of Easton's Books, Mount Vernon, WA. Thanks to Billie Swift, Gabrielle Bates, Kym Littlefield, and Alexander Moysaenko of Open Books, Seattle, WA (and former owners, Christine Deavel and John Marshall). Thanks to the team at Ristretto Coffee for providing a space for meetings.

Thanks for hosting pre-publication reading events: MoNA in La Conner, The Mount Vernon Public Library, and Village Books. Thanks for the generosity of your opening statements Mayors Jill Boudreau (Mount Vernon) and Ramon Hayes (La Conner).

Thanks to our kind and generous donors—particularly those who funded the Mary Malyon Brose Seed Fund, and those who sponsored our April 2017 Juvenile Justice Issues Event. Thanks to all the crew at Tierra Nueva for the space to create the initial version of our ongoing vision. Thanks to David Westerlund for connections and camaraderie. Thanks to Kera Wanielista, *Skagit Valley Herald*, for letting people know about our work.

Thanks to all the groups who have hosted Underground Writing speaking engagements and trainings.

Thanks to Nathan McGehee for designing our beautiful cover!

Thanks to Alvin Shim for your multi-faceted communications work—social media, film, photography, and *The Underground Writing Podcast*. So very grateful for your work with us.

Thanks to Jennifer Morison Hendrix for all your time and effort in ordering, formatting, and copy editing.

Thanks to Quiara Alegría Hudes for the Foreword to *What No One Ever Tells You*, partnership via Emancipated Stories, making the New York City trip in April 2018 happen (thanks, too, Ford Foundation and Elizabeth Alexander!), and your support and enthusiasm for our work. You've been a great encouragement to our program and students.

Endless gratitude to Underground Writing's devoted and passionate Teaching Writers: A. Muia, Chris Hoke, Jennifer Bradbury, Jennifer Morison Hendrix, Matt Malyon, and Susanne Paola Antonetta. Our program is infinitely better because we're on this journey together.

Shout-outs and thanks! to all our students. You have moved, challenged, and inspired us beyond what you can know. May your voices continue to rise. May you grow increasingly aware of the importance of what you have to say and give to the world. May you continue to use writing as part of this.

Partners

EMANCIPATED STORIES

Are you incarcerated?

Do you want to emancipate a piece of your story?

Share a part of yourself, set it free.

WHAT IS IT?
Our goal is to collect one page from every person behind bars in this country. Each page will be unique, a testimony to a life. Alone, each page means, "I am here." Together, all the pages mean, "We are here."

WHERE IS IT?
Find us on Instagram at @emancipated_stories_project. Eventually we may create a book, or public readings, or visual exhibits.

HOW CAN I PARTICIPATE?

Your page may be a drawing, a letter, a poem, a story, an essay, a lyric.

Mail your page to:

Emancipated Stories
809 West 181st Street, Box 146
New York NY 10033

Or email the page to emancipatedstories@gmail.com

EMANCIPATED STORIES
FAQ

Who can submit?
Currently and formerly incarcerated people.

What can I submit?
Drawings, essays, letters, stories, poems. Black and white or color. Limited to one page.

Will I get credit for my work?
Yes, if you include your name. Include your address, and we'll keep you posted with updates. Anonymous submissions are accepted, too.

I have a poem or drawing I already created. Can I submit that?
Yes.

I have a poem or drawing that was already published. Can I submit that?
If it's ok with the other publisher, yes.

My loved one is in prison and sent me a letter, poem, or work of art. Can I submit that?
Please get their permission before sending a submission on their behalf.

How do I see the Emancipated Stories?
We will go live on Instagram in September 2017.

What topics are you looking for?
Anything. A snippet of your life, a moment from your day, a memory, a dream...

Is there any censorship involved with this project?
We do not censor content just because it's intense. We encourage truthful submissions on all topics, of all tones. However, if content seems inappropriate for internet publication we will let you know.

Is someone making money off this?
Nope. This is strictly a volunteer project.

Who started this?
Quiara Alegría Hudes, a Pulitzer-winning playwright, and her cousin Sean Ortiz who is currently serving time in a federal correction facility. Others have joined our journey including Eddie Torres, a theater artist and former Criminal Defense Investigator with 20 years experience in Capital Post conviction cases; May Treuhaft-Ali, a student and literary scholar; and Armando Riesco, an actor who translated our original flier into Spanish.

Brigid Collins Family Support Center is a commitment-based organization causing the end of child abuse. When one child is hurt, it means the child, their family, and our community need healing. We envision a world that cares for and nurtures all of its children and share a dedication to this vision's fulfillment. We invite others to join us in this work.

Originally founded in Bellingham, Washington in 1990, Brigid Collins Family Support Center is the legacy of a core group of volunteers who had a hope of better coordinating the community's response to child sexual abuse. Today, we have grown to serve more than 2,000 families each year throughout the Northwest corner of Washington. We continue to carry out our original mission by coordinating the Children's Advocacy Centers in both Whatcom and Skagit Counties and working closely with all local law enforcement jurisdictions, prosecuting attorneys, medical providers, child protection workers and therapists from both counties.

Our dream has grown. Instead of responding to just child sexual abuse, we have a comprehensive vision of a world in which every child is nurtured, and child abuse and neglect cease to exist.

Skagit County
917 S. 3rd St.
Mount Vernon, WA 98273
428-6622
contact@brigidcollins.org

Whatcom County
1231 N. Garden St. #200
Bellingham, WA 98225
734-4616
contact@brigidcollins.org

The Mount Vernon Migrant Leaders Club prepares middle and high school migrant students for college and career by cultivating youth voice and leadership. In a safe, student-driven environment, club members create opportunities for personal expression, giving the students the opportunity to see themselves and be seen by others as emerging leaders.

Janice Blackmore, Club Advisor/Migrant Graduation Specialist
Mount Vernon School District
1200 North LaVenture Road
Mount Vernon, WA 98273
360.428.6116
jblackmore@mvsd320.org

YMCA Oasis Daylight Center will have fun activities, food and a computer lab for teens 13-17 years old. Staff will be there to help with homework, build a resume, search for jobs and more. Each day there will be different activities such as painting, games, crafts, cooking, LGTBQ support and more.

Supported by The Jack & Shirley McIntyre Foundation

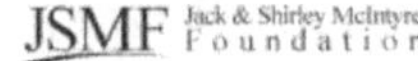

Our Oasis Daylight Program offers a safe place for community teens to gather during the day that includes meals, arts and crafts, educational workshops, and a computer lab for vocational and academic support. Different activities are offered each day, so be sure to check our current schedule.

We are excited to announce that, thanks to support from the McIntyre family, the YMCA Oasis Daylight Center (ODLC) has its doors open to community teens ages 13-17. This program is free, and youth do not need to be homeless or at-risk to access this program. This means that shelter and community teens have a safe place to gather during the day that will include meals, arts and crafts, educational workshops, and a computer lab for vocational and academic support.

The support from the community has been outstanding. Many agencies, parents, and retired professionals have volunteered to spend time at Oasis mentoring, playing games, and supporting our youth. To name a few agencies that will be providing support to teens at Oasis: WorkSource, Planned Parenthood, Catholic Community Services/Community Services, PFLAG, Goodwill, Skagit Domestic Violence & Sexual Assault Services, and the Mount Vernon Library. The collaboration continues, and we are ready to rumble!

YMCA OASIS Daylight Center
125 N 5th St, Mount Vernon, WA 98273
360.419.9058
http://www.skagitymca.org/oasis-daylight-center

Skagit County Juvenile Detention

Mission Statement

Skagit County Juvenile Detention will provide a safe and secure environment for all residents. All admissions will be carefully screened pursuant to the Revised Code of Washington (RCW) and to administrative guidelines. Procedures and policies will be in line with RCW, case law, court rules, constitutional rights and human rights. Consideration for the rights and feelings of parents/guardians will also be a priority. An educational program as mandated by RCW will be provided.

This facility is committed to going beyond RCW mandates. We are committed to providing detention structure and programs aimed at teaching residents how to control and modify their behavior. Programs offered in detention cover a wide variety of topics, but all are aimed at expanding the resident's view of his/her world. The goal is, in conjunction with community probation and parole, to enhance the youth's chances of a successful re-entry into the community.

611 South Second Street
Mount Vernon, WA 98273-3820
360.416.1230
https://www.skagitcounty.net

Skagit County Community Justice Center

The Skagit County Sheriff's Office Corrections Division is an around the clock, 24/7 operation. Currently 52 Corrections Deputies, 10 Corrections Sergeants, and 1 Lieutenant are responsible for providing safe and secure housing for inmates being held in the custody of the Skagit County Jail.

The staff of the jail is also responsible for inmate movement outside of the jail facility, such as court appearances, medical appointments, etc. In addition to the Division's in-house responsibilities, Corrections staff are responsible for peripheral duties, which include Medical Liaison, Jail Billing, Court Security, and the Jail Alternatives Program.

The Jail Alternatives Program offers alternatives to standard methods of incarceration for those who qualify. Such alternatives include Work Release, Community Service Work, and Electronic Home Monitoring. Further, the Corrections Division employs one civilian working as the Division's Court Coordinator, responsible for facilitating the resolution of cases with multiple charges from multiple jurisdictions.

201 Suzanne Lane
Mount Vernon, WA 98273
(360) 416-1960
FAX: (360) 336-9390

Founded in July 2015, Underground Writing is a literature-based creative writing program serving migrant, incarcerated, recovery, and other at-risk communities in northern Washington through literary engagement and personal restoration. We facilitate generative encounters with literature spanning the tradition—from ancient texts to those written in our workshops. Honoring the transforming power of the word, we believe that attentive reading leads to attentive writing, and that attentive writing has the power to assist in the restoration of communities, the imagination, and individual lives.

For information regarding programs, speaking and consulting, volunteering, or donations, please contact us.

Underground Writing
P.O. Box 1043
Mount Vernon, WA 98273
360.220.0467

e | info@undergroundwriting.org
w | www.undergroundwriting.org

Workshop Sites
Migrant Leaders Club—Mount Vernon School District
Skagit County Community Justice Center
Skagit County Juvenile Detention
Skagit Valley Recovery Community
YMCA Oasis Daylight Center